WE SPEAK

Voices from Chattanooga's Disregarded

from Seven Monologue Plays
by
Peggy Douglas

Illustrations by Mark Making's Art Class Participants
from Various Hamilton County (TN) Detention Centers
and the Hamilton County Mental Health Court
Sexual Trauma Tract Program

Acknowledgements

First, I would like to express my gratitude for the stouthearted souls who shared their personal histories and allowed me to transform their stories into dramatic monologues for the stage.

I would like to thank Ray Zimmerman for his judicious editing of this publication; as well as Jann Sullivan, Marilyn Sizer, and David Cook for their valuable assistance and support in writing this collection of poetic monologues that have been performed in the following plays:

UnMasking: Elders Speak: Oral Histories of Chattanoogans (2023). Barking Legs Theater.
https://www.youtube.com/watch?v=CVGYggmY58A&t=35s

Unmasking: Beyond the Rainbow: Queer Remembrances (2023). Barking Legs Theater.
https://www.youtube.com/watch?app=desktop&v=PyT8ytQ6ogQ&feature=youtu.be

UnMasking: Now We Speak: Stories from the Incarcerated (2022). ArtsBuild Chattanooga.
https://www.youtube.com/watch?v=zzvhgbfJux8&t=100s

Steel Toes and Hired Hands: Stories from Domestics, Working Class and Hired Hands (2021). Miller Park, Chattanooga.
https://www.youtube.com/watch?v=v0_O2JjRlqc&t=2s

Southern Exposure: Growing Up Southern (2020). McCoy Farms and Garden. https://www.wutc.org/post/southern-exposure-heard-wutc

Deeper Roots: Stories from Walden's Ridge, TN (2019). Backman Community Center.

A special thanks to the Tennessee Arts Commission, Humanities TN, ArtsBuild, Mark Making, the Mountain Arts Center, and Barking Legs for their funding and partnerships.

I would also like to acknowledge the numerous actors and the following directors who brought the monologues to life on the stage: Anne Swedberg, Trish Ross, Dennis Parker, and Ryan Laskowski.

For my children: Jimmy and Frances; my grandchildren: Abby, Ally, Alex, and Liam; my sisters: Caroline, Jann, Julie, Lynn, Andrea, Barbara, Nancy, Gray, Frances M., Anne, Tracy, Pat, and Deb,

and in memory of my mama, Maggie Bell.

Contents

from Southern Exposure

from Chattanooga Elders

The Incarcerated

The Baker

All my life, I have tried to make bread
by burying trouble beneath the surface
and praying for a bountiful loaf to rise, as if
tainted loaves would break ground like wheat
in the spring. offering blessings of hope
and tranquility.

My loaves are made of a lifetime of secrets--
the men who put their hands on me, beat me,
left me for dead, and all the days I cooked
and crooked, got caught with my hands
in the dough.

Those loaves hold all my father's drunken
rages, all my mother's worried edges. Oh, how
I longed to smooth the river of her. But I am
the daughter who sold drugs, who traded my soul
for an 8-ball and two fifths of Jim Beam.
My bread, unearthed from some forgotten meth
kitchen, was dark, moldy and full of rotten
memories.

Before I got to prison, the drugs and booze
had eaten the hand that feeds me, then the arm,
the elbow, the shoulder. Hell, it had eaten my whole
body alive until I heard the ending to my story —
a plastic tarp and a plush ride to the morgue.

But now, in these prison walls,
a little while dry, a little while with no
chattering chimp between my ears, I fall
upon my knees and plead to God, Please
deliver me from the desires that fire the night
with infinite longing.

What I want you to know about me
is: I am strong and I have hope and faith
that after my release, I will be graced by a fresh
loaf that steams when I slice it, leavened
by the clean air I breathe.

Orphan Girl

You might wonder what an angelic looking
twenty-two-year-old is doing in jail, possibly spending
most of my life behind prison bars instead of out hunting
ginseng and bloodroot. Well, I wish I could give you
a simple answer.

What I want you to know about me is: I am scared —
of depression, my unknown future, and mean girls
in the next bunk whose words cut deep. These concrete
prison walls look like the sea at night, hard and endless.

You should also know that I am all about the woods,
but in Silverdale, I cannot hear birds or go outside
to see fall tree colors or a daylily bloom. Ever since
I was little, I loved to go barking, not like wild dogs,
but like an archeologist who ventures into the woods
for treasure-- witch hazel bark which brings four dollars
a pound in town.

My childhood memories are jumbled up
with a father who chose the local bar each night
rather than his daughter who waited up for the chance
he'd come home and sing just one karaoke song with her--
a song that never came. Shortly after he left for good,
my mother abandoned me and my little brother
on a Rhea County highway so she could start over
in Alabama.

I started over, too, in homeless shelters, church halls,
and occasionally on someone's couch. It wasn't long
before I fell in with an old man who sold me out for drugs
to feed his addiction and turned me on to meth so I could bury
my own disappointments. My drugging days ended
one night, when I hit another car head-on, killing
my passenger and injuring five others.

That day rolls over in my mind as I try to sleep.
I feel so alone and tired of living in the past. If I look back
straight (which is not the same as remembering) at my orphaning —
arriving at school in Goodwill clothes, an odd odor

of abandonment, chapped face and hands uncaressed
by a loved one, I am lost until I drift back to a steamy
hot day when I set off into the woods, hunting nature's
bounty to trade for an evening meal.

I am not afraid of forest shadows or the clash
of thunder, what lightning can do. What I fear most
is being kept away from flowers and rivers, from valleys
and mountains, from trees and seas that I can't see
from this windowless theater. In my restless sleep,
the branches I once bent to find my way home
have disappeared.

So, like Now and its friend Then, I avoid thinking
of my mama who once tucked me in, saying, *don't worry,*
everything will be okay. I know she didn't believe her words,
but I cling to them just the same. I have a tattoo that reads,
Stay the course. How does that work you might ask?

 I steady on with the Rock of Ages Bible Study
(answered 252 questions last night), play Christian music
on my headphones all day, and pray:

> *The fear inside will flee.*
> *I will have a breakthrough today.*
> *My circumstances will change.*

I follow the impulse that lures me to those promises
and can almost see the forest's witch hazel and ginseng,
even the ivy and itch — those gentle words that whisper:
eat, sleep, gather, love, pray, and have faith, telling me
to cradle hope until I can return to the life
I have yet to create.

Pure Gravy

What I want you to know about me
is that I am beautiful. But used to be — a lost
woman who fell in love with men full of lechery
so solid you could build a table on it. For years,
I chose the man to suit the instant, and when
each left me for dead, the blues would camp out
inside me for weeks at a time. So I learned to drink
and drug and forget the ones who filled my soul
with hollow invitations. My story is one of being alone,
even among friends and lovers.

But listen and I'll tell you the story
about the morning my life changed: I wake up
in an alley, a world surrounded by brick.
Through a window across the way, a man's face
pops up as if to study my stalled sexuality.
His stay is brief. Then another face. The men take turns,
Pushing and shoving, for the slightest sight of me.
I said I would never be like them — those women
who freely turn tricks for a quarter gram of coke,
yet here I am. I wasn't bought or sold into street life,
I was birthed into it — abused by my uncle in third grade
and afraid to tell my mother. My fate was written
on the day I was born. Those men in the window know —
I am theirs for the taking… and leaving.

For years, I have offered strangers moments
of pleasure. You could say, I am in the business
of pleasure, but that's an irony. The numerous scars
littering my body never saw an ounce of delight.
In those dark red years of hopeless fate, my defiant
soul was my only escape. Here on the streets, things cost
a lot. The fat cat businessmen hurry by us on their way to
work, as if we are unsavory, canceling any history
of the night before. Looking up at the men in the window,
I cry out — *please Lord, send help.*

And it came — the 5-year prison sentence finally shut
the door to my body, and provided years to reflect
and pray: *Let me cease to fear the embrace that longs
to still me.* That's when I learned healing can be deep

as the wound that binds me. With God's grace,,
I became a loose- petaled poppy, blown open,
in tune with the earth's heartbeat. I was released
early, with a knowing, I wasn't gonna yield to any
random voice that demanded: *let me in*. And my family,
my sweet family eventually forgave me and I forgave
them for being what I was not. Blessed are they that
remember what they now have, they longed for.

Today, all I can say is *Gravy*. For that's what my life is.
Alive, three years clean and sober, working a meaningful job,
surrounded by a loving family when nobody expected me
to be alive this long. Pure gravy, I tell you.

Mama's Boy

What I want you to know about me is:
I am my mama's boy. You may not think it
by my tough exterior, but inside, I am a jelly roll
who believes in love and kindness, just like Mama
taught me, although I've backslid a few times
on the twisty road to get here.

Let me take you back to the time when I was eight
and my sister and me ran loose through shops and arcades
at the Whitfield County mall while Mama worked
back-to-back jobs at Payless and American Cookie Company.
I'm the one with the trendy look that Mama doesn't need
to fuss over— short braids on top, the rest shaved
all around.

Now in that mall, I am a poser with my Samuel L. Jackson
stance, hands deep in pockets of long bulky jeans, a ratty,
natty hand-me-down shirt in Black Panther cross colors,
topped off with oversized knock-off Air Jordans. You might
think I'd stand out, but I know how to vanish into the dark
chamber of the arcade, that dungeon where I dare to fight
demons and dragons all day, where only the Saturday Night
Street Fighter, King Rasta, can see me, grab me, jump
straight up about 15 feet while backflipping a dozen times,
then throw me straight down to the mat. I enjoy that—
just to see how he can do it, that swagger he packs
in his victory shrug.

After I turned ten, Mama let me roam the streets
where fighting was real, where my stepbrothers and me
skipped school, hopped trains, and crushed our rivals.
My mama hoped I would survive that life without totaling
myself but I was the clown in my family's act whose downfall
began when I highjacked a car at age twelve that ended
in a crash which took my friend's life and sent me to juvenile
jail for vehicular manslaughter.

I remember sitting in that small intake room, listening
to the clatter inside my head, *you idiot, you idiot, you idiot*,
eyes lowered, not looking up or down, thinking if I moved,
I'd break apart. It went on like that until one night

I dreamed my mama was patting my shoulder
with that tender, spirited hand motioning me to turn
my back on the street life full of troublemakers. That's when
I promised myself to quit holding combat in high regard.

During those years of detention, her picture hung on my wall
and called up memories. Closing my eyes, I smelled the aroma
of shepherd's pie in her kitchen, tasted the double doozie cookies
she brought home from work, and felt the beauty and ugliness
of a hard and painful childhood that could be soothed by a mama
with bright eyes and her words: *When you're in a hole, hand yourself
a rope and climb out of it.* Looking at her photo, I searched her pupils
for a path to peace and imagined her deliberately waiting for me
to come home. Sometimes in my dreams she came to me.

Come here, she said. Let me sing you a song
so you can learn to find hope as you have borne pain.
> *Now hold on, your change is coming.*
> *Hold on, don't worry 'bout a thing.*
> *Hold on, everything will be alright.*
> ~~ Tupac Shakur

.

Shifters and Boppers

Viva Las Vegas

Larry Larimore did not die a glorious death at the Soya
vegetable oil refinery in Chattanooga. He didn't explode
in a fireball as the spark of a welder's torch ignited solvent fumes.
He was not sheared by the claws of rail cars coupling in the yard,
Nor did he trip and slide on oil slick floors or lose an arm
from unprotected machinery and moving parts. He did not fall
into half-full grain silos or get speared by a hung-over fork lift operator.
Larry Larimore simply lowered his union coffee mug one morning,
dropped his head and went out like a flame.

Thinking he had just dozed off, we prodded him
with a pencil eraser tip as we passed by, silenced
the control alarms on his sound board during the day.
Only when Larry's relief showed up did we realize
he was gone. So today, at the gravesite, I give my brief
eulogy:

Refinery men, in general, are easy to like. Bland, as he could be,
Larry was an open book. You never know what a man will tell a young
female co-worker who is not his wife. I don't care if the stories
were true, Larry's moments of revelation were warm and tender.

The closest thing Larry had to a hobby was Ann-Margret.
I tell you what, "Lucy, he said to me, that star looks better
at fifty than you in your twenties. Remember her movie
where Bette Davis is a homeless old drunk who writes
letters to her daughter who is Ann-Margret pretending
to be a high society lady. Bette Davis pulls it off to the end.
It's the only movie I ever saw where lying was the best policy."

The fact is when you strip away Larry's blandness,
there is more blandness, even in his death. Alls I could say
at his funeral was, "Larry loved Ann-Margret." His wife, Shirley,
gave me a look like, one more crack about Ann-Margret
and I'll knock your block off.

I'm thinking there's no way Shirley can understand the reference.
It's not like she had any idea who Larry Larimore was. But just as
I'm about to totally dismiss Larry's widow, she turns to the band
and hollers, "play Viva Las Vegas for Larry and Ann-Margret."

Mill Village (from Deb Clardy)

I haven't owned the things most women crave--
the touch of silk, perfumes and jewels, but I've caressed
dewdrops in the morning light, felt the warm sun's
breath rise, and the comfort of tender friendships
in this old mill village.

You might have noticed me--the warm, cheerful
woman in a worn nightie, face wrinkled with age,
leaning out my kitchen window with a cigarette stub
squeezed tight between teeth as I take communion
from a casual breeze. I blow trouble away through smoke
hole after hole, until my thoughts turn to what I treasure —
family, friends, dogs, and of course, my gardens.

This morning, I'm sitting on the back porch,
facing Mama Clardy's rose bush, gazing across the field
where the old mill stood tall above our village community,
dirtying it, smoking it like unfiltered cigarettes, covering up
gardens with smog and foul odor. It's gone now but I can
still picture the pale-faced mill workers every evening
trudging past me to make third shift.

Yes, some of the stories about mill life were true.
Like the boss who, without regard or pity, imposed
the Stretch-out, a back-breaking pace that left workers sick
and weak. Faster and louder the machines would roar,
as specks of lint swirled and floated, draping hair
and eyelashes, crawling up their noses, down throats,
into their lungs. At the time, lint dust was like smoking.
Nobody thought much about it.

If you'd asked her, Mama Clardy would say she loved
every minute of those years as a mill girl, probably stayed
if the arthritis hadn't caught up with her. *We had some good
days, steady days,* she'd say, *when the dust had time to settle.*
To Mama Clardy, the Village was more than the mill.
It was a community of decent houses full of good,
moral people.

I tended to Mama Clardy at night before she reached
the other side. You don't sleep in a chair by a death bed,
but you do dream-- old Village stories weaving their way
through my mind. She never expected such a crowd
at her funeral, but they all came. The Village is a place
that believes in honoring its living and dead-- welcomes
all as family—whether newly arrived or long gone buried.
The night she died, stray dogs barked the distance between row
houses like old friends calling out across a field they're too tired
to cross, and the stories of mill families swirled like lint dust,
until the history of a woman became the history of village.

I wouldn't have traded my life for all the riches in Scotland.
I have set my body solidly upon this village, rooted my head
to its sky, and my feet in the depths of its soil, just like the old
white oak in the front yard. That tree reminds me of how
happiness is delicately woven day by day, and how it's not
sudden and it's not constant. Inside the bark is growing
even though you can't see it. The tree is lifted by this inward
work, until its branches shine and its leaves glitter.

Free Groceries

In high school, my boyfriend Larry worked at the A&P,
stocking shelves on Fridays until midnight. Then he'd drive
to my house, sneak me out and carry me down to the tracks
by the cotton mill where he lifted me and the quilt I carried
into an empty boxcar. He danced me to the thundering sounds
of looms, the roar of trains passing on adjacent tracks hauling
cotton bales or rolls of muslin on their way to the bleachery
to be whitened, patterned into stripes and checks, or still-life
gardens of wisteria and rose.

I remember the night we listened to the year-end countdown
on my transistor radio. Heartbeat Hotel by Elvis is #1 on WFLI.
Larry always picks the Big Jet Fly over WLAC, the night-time blues
station for half the nation. Personally, I like Little Anthony
and the Imperials, Sam Cooke, and how Johnny Mathis sings
about love. But Larry fancies Elvis, sings Jailhouse Rock
nodding his noggin like bobblehead doll, his smile spreading
over us like a cold we're almost happy to have. Sometimes,
we dance to the slow ones in heavy boots and coats,
our breath filling the air with moist heat. And when the whistle
signals the end of third shift, Larry lifts me down to the gravel
and takes me home.

If my mother ever knew, she didn't say, so grateful for the bags
of damaged goods stolen from the stockroom and mysteriously left
on our kitchen table. Slashed bags of rice and beans he bandaged
with masking tape, cans without labels, cereals and detergents
in varying stages of destruction, but plenty enough to help us
get by for the week. Some Saturday mornings, we might even find
some plums and cherries, tender and delicious, still whole inside
the mutilated cans, floating in their own sweet juice.

The Resurrectionist

A guy wearing a tie and a soaked shirt was spewing
out religious rubbish on Market Street today, asking passersby
if they'd been saved from eternal damnation by Christ,
our personal lord and savior. I'd just picked up four cows
at the city feedlot and my mind was on carting the load
to the Armour meat-processing plant, dreaming of quitting time
when I could settle back with a cold one and the World Series.

But the preacher came over, wearing enough cheap cologne
to keep a dog away from a fresh bone, asked if I knew where
I'd go when I die and if I believed in that resurrection business.
I thought of the farmer's dead palomino he had me carry off
last week and told that preacher I wasn't sure about heaven
or hell, but I worked in resurrection, too. Even so, I had no
time to compare stories as my load needed to reach the slaughter
house on Cowart Street before it closed.

Who is he to ask me where I'm going when I die?
Me and that preacher and a millionaire will end up drained,
pickled and dressed in suits, and that's all any of us knows.
What's left is just a lifeless carcass the undertaker powders
and buries instead of hauling it off to the rendering plant.
That undertaker and me both save the dead from piling up.
People would know if somebody wasn't here to keep dead
horses from laying around getting ripe after they died.

I don't need to imagine more of a heaven than the cool
nights along Chickamauga Creek when largemouth bass pop
the surface and bite on anything you throw, or watching quail
break from a field of cornstalks, or even having Rhonda call me *Darlin'*
when I stop for lunch at Nikki's Drive-In. I won't say I'm ready.
But if I get run over by a tobacco truck tonight, I'll die knowing
I did some good in life, that I was willing to do a job most folks
wouldn't even consider.

The Appalachians

Mama's Passing

I knew she was sick-- my Mama, who fried boneyards
of chicken in a lifetime, and was known to sneak a powder
and play Boil them Cabbage Down on the banjo so fast
the fiddlers had to lay their bows to rest. I remember
the times she let me sleep at the foot of her spindle bed
so we could listen to the Philco, as I drifted off to the tinny
voices of Jimmy Rodgers, Pop Stoneman, and the Carter
family.

Not many folk are here to pay respect, just the weighty few-
the old drunk who recalled Mama's merciful glass of
buttermilk, the women who rocked on the front porch
with her-- cutting okra, coddling grandbabies, and spinning
bawdy lies. Folk with grease under nails that no amount
of Octagon soap can set free. People of the pines.
My people.

I've always been suspicious about God. But today,
when I look at her sweet, peaceful body in the open
coffin, thin hands across full breasts, I imagine her spirit
up there with Him, blowing a hurricane on the harmonica
and singing a little too loud. I look around at my family
and remember what Mama said about family life being precious—
the love of Uncle Earl who hauled us kids to the ice cream parlor
on Friday nights, Aunt Bessie who picked bones out of my fried
crappie so I wouldn't choke, and my mama's Cousin Jimmy
who drove a 1931 Nash Single Six with a naked lady hood
ornament that mortified his wife so bad, she painted
a bathing suit over the chrome body. And the matriarch
of it all, my granny who once pulverized a six-foot rattlesnake
with a Steven's Favorite 22.

I think about all the wisdom Mama laid on me.
She always said that nobody wants to hear the TRUTH,
but everyone wants a story. So, Mama, this one's for you.

Life's Journey

Gales have been blowing across Walden's Ridge
for years. Families abandoned mines, farms, and cotton mills.
Tradition is graying like our cedar trees. Sometimes, I wonder
if we'll survive progress. But today, I noticed a small spider
rebuilding a home, rinsing dust from her face. Look closely,
you can learn from her, see as she sees.

Watch the spider's web there, whose hinges reel heavily
and crazily with the dust, whole mounds and cemeteries of it,
sagging and scattering shadows among landscape. Notice
as she steps into the center of air, slender and fastidious,
the golden hair of daylight along her shoulders. She's poised there,
while ruins crumble on every side of her, free of the dust,
as though she had just stepped onto the earth to bathe herself.

Walden's Ridge, like chiggers and corn liquor, is everlasting.
It'll always be, though not always as we remember. Our past rusts
peels, but never fades away. I can still see my maternal great
grandmother, Willadean, go at a copperhead with a hoe held together
with black electrical tape; it never had a chance. My great grandfather,
John, worked 12 hours mining coal, six more with his hands
in rocky clay. My Uncle John wore out 15 straw hats and worked
three mules to death. Now it's is my turn, to curse the drought,
the late spring frost, the rocks in the earth.

I gaze closer until she steps away in her own good time.
Many folks have searched all over Walden's Ridge and never
sensed what I found in that spider's web, the heart of light itself,
balancing on filaments. The secret of this journey is to allow
the wind to blow its dust all over your body, to let it go
and step lightly, all the way through your ruins, and not to lose
any sleep over the dead, who surely rest in peace.

Lumberjacks

It sounds like something that's been told
too many times, but I want you to know,
there are no men around today like those
when I was a young lumberjack. You might see
these enormous old tree stumps with notches
on the side, and not think *those were some big
ass trees.*

You might imagine what men do with logging
machines today is hard work, but we used it all
by hand. We did it all standing on springy, narrow boards,
stuck twelve feet up above the ground, sometimes
with canyons below us, swinging our axes
into hard wood.

To move along the tree tops, we'd give a hop
with one toe held under the springboard to swing it.
Then we'd stick the axe in the wood and stoop
to reach our saws. I never saw or heard of one who fell,
but once a man turned to reach for his saw
and brushed that razor-sharp axe. It slit his middle
right along the belt line for about eight inches, so wide
his intestines looped down like bunting. When they came
with the stretcher this man was crouched on his knees
delicately holding up his gut loops one by one splashing
sawdust off them with water from his waterbag.
So I'm telling you — there are no men like that today.

Waking the Dead

I sit on the porch steps, and watch my daddy
lean his hefty body against the back of Uncle
Leroy's wagon. In the background, a mushroom
rock rises, looming like an anchored rain cloud.
Cousin Buddy crouches next to a wagon wheel
right hand knuckling the swept dirt yard.
My older brother stands nearby, cross armed,
like all of 'em--- proud of today's accomplishment.

Loud enough to wake the dead, Granny hissed
as their fingers rattled front door hinges. Barging in
uninvited, they muddied her freshly mopped floor
and flung open the bedroom door. Entering the
darkened room, they shared news of their great luck
with my granddaddy, twelve rod-doubling trout
caught that morning along the banks of North
Chickamauga Creek.

Words finally weren't enough. They slung
the bedpan into the corner, tumbled sheets to the floor,
gripping wasted flesh between them, as they dragged
my granddaddy, barefoot and pajamaed into a sultry
July afternoon. In the oak tree's mighty shade,
they opened the fish-gorged ice box, worried a rainbow
of flies, measured, re-counted each fish story, arguing
worms vs. corn, silk vs. cotton lines.

They would not leave until Granny came out
and acknowledged the moment, a slight nod,
then shook her pointer finger, one-eyed at those
who dared disturb the dying. Years later, I can still see
granddaddy's face, a slight grin behind that cigarette,
so content with family and a simple life. But amidst our
hardships, there's a sweetness that dwells on this mountain.
It's the one sure thing I know.

Winter Greens

Age and late winter stiffened your stoop
as you gathered wild greens from the creek bed,
before rinsing the grit in spring water. How long
they simmered I don't know. You didn't speak
to me as a child— a sternness made formal by poverty.
Perhaps you thought me weak, loving books and pen
over hunting and fishing. Or perhaps you knew
I preferred the company of women—aunts and grannies,
all the abundance that permits warmth and levity
over men who carry the weight of each refused tear.

You died before I was grown, long before I knew
how the sediment of solitude can silt a lifespan
like yours or mine, the way a small pond fills
with algae and cattails. Cleaning my own greens,
I hold their bodies in loose embrace, as thoughts
of cooking and kinship roll back and forth under knife,
removing the stringy filaments.

But see here, papa— though we share blood and bone,
I am what happens when God lives between pages
of books, on tips of pencils, the sharp edges
of writing paper. I am of women, too.

Queer Voices

Coming Out Further

I stand by my girlfriend, Jane, at Daddy's funeral.
In her platform sneakers, she towers over the row
of grieving family members who receive outstretched
arms and condolences. We are last in line but nobody
comes near, passing us by with piercing looks.

My Aunt Pearl—the one who changed my diapers,
Godmothered and carried me to the playground
with her son Bobby throughout our childhood, mumbles
as she finally shuffles past me. *Say what?* I asked her.
*Heart attack, not in a million years; He couldn't handle
the shame of his lesbian daughter. That's what killed him.*
I whispered to Jane, *it definitely wasn't the two-pack-a-day
habit and cases of Jim Beam.*

The funeral was the last time I saw my daddy's family.
I'm ready to rediscover my voice and I plan to use it.
I want to become the old hound sitting on the back stoop
howling all night because she wants to, the young girl
climbing the tall wooden fence because it's there,
the woman who will take another's hand when it is offered,
kiss the knuckles of each finger, and drink from the ripe
opening of her eyes.

Last night, I dreamed of a new career, imagining
life in a small congregation of queer Episcopalians
somewhere in the Northeast, a rural town not known
for tolerance, but respectful, even a bit in awe of something
that passes for different and exciting. In that dream,
I am their priest, their good shepherd and all my flock
plays musical instruments and gives fabulous dinner parties.

That is the life I imagine myself in, waving my pretend
baton, conducting the band that doesn't exist, living
in the town I may never even visit. But that dream isn't real.
So I'm staying put. Maybe even coming out further. Ha!
Aunt Pearl, come meet my wife.

Wasted Hot Dogs

I pity the fools who buy perfectly good packs
of wieners and drive around Chattanooga
chucking them at homos while yelling, "*Pansy*"
in unison. And then the cowards speed off--
missing the point, the pleasure of the attack.
Dear bigots, you should have seen the hot dog hit
the scarf Tommy sewed from an antique silk
kimono: so gay. You missed laughing at us, your
raw hot dog limp on the ground.

Did you hurt me and Tommy? Don't you know,
we make fun of such bigots as I wash the scarf
in Woolite while Tommy sings, *tall and tan and young
and lovely, the girl from Ipanema goes walking....*
Do we think twice about you? Listen, we worry
about dates and how to spend our allowance,
not Oscar Mayers fired from jacked-up King cabs.
We decided many years ago to leave the idea
of hate out on the streets when we go inside.

In downtown Chattanooga, it sometimes rains
hot dogs, because we are everywhere; there's nowhere
else for us, or you, to go. But I'm telling you this
right now: Anywhere you drive around in this town,
love will be there to greet you. And around any corner,
there might be two men. Kissing. So, you better stock
up.

Trans Man

Are you kidding me? I raised you to be a strong feminist.
How can you go to the other side? my mother cried when I came out
as trans. Dad just shrugged, *you'll never look like Arnold Schwarzenegger.*
Listen, my parents are cool but they definitely traversed the trans
learning curve before they got to acceptance. But that's their story.

This is mine. When I was younger, I awoke most mornings
feeling small and terrified. I couldn't find myself in my own life.
There was no place outside of me where I belonged. So every morning
I had to will myself back into existence. I strained to look into my future,
trying to picture the road ahead of me, searching for a glimpse
of who I would become.

I think the transition started when I was 13 and got into Cosplay —
a performance art where participants called cosplayers wear costumes
and fashion accessories to represent a specific character. I always chose
to be a male character. When I got to college, I met a trans guy
named Chris who already had top surgery and was taking hormones.
He inspired me to start using male pronouns, binding, and packing.
At 19, I told my mom that I was ready to start masculinizing
hormone therapy, but I was scared to do it on my own. She initially
protested my taking the hormones, but she and Dad eventually
came on board.

You might think I had a lot of motivation for transitioning
But surrendering is unimaginably more dangerous than struggling
for survival. Making the gender transition was like rushing into a burning
building to discover how to live my own life. It took a while
before I began to feel pleasure in the airy state between here and there.
I'm not saying I'll live to see some sort of paradise. It is still hard.
But if I hadn't walked this path, who would I be? How would I know
courage, which is not just living through a nightmare, it's doing
something with it afterwards. It's being brave enough to talk
about it with others. Today, I live proudly in a body
of my own design, and I defend my right to be complex.

Words

You won't go to hell for it, Honey. Being a lesbian
is a reversable sin, my high school guidance counselor,
Miss Peale, told me. *Think of it like having clubbed feet*
when you're born. Almost all children who get early treatment
are able to run and play quite normally. You just need to pray
hard to change your evil thoughts. I remember what my Nana
promising that sticks and *stones break bones but words can't hurt.*
Ha. Miss Peale's words shoved me into a closet full of self-loathing
and terror. I was a dandelion in a field of flowers who could pretend
to be a rose but I knew deep down that I was a thistle.

I'd heard whispers of people like me-- names like butch,
bull dagger, dike. So on the bus ride home that day, I stuffed
my shame under the dry, cracked leather seats so as not to carry it
in the house. You see, I am not the daughter my mother ordered.
I wouldn't tell her I was falling, a breathless tumbling dance t
hat contained who I am as I entered a cave of loneliness.

No wound hurts like the silence of those who watch our flesh
sliced open or simply mop up our spilled blood so that it won't
dirty the dawn. *But I'm a good person*, I cried once alone
in my room. I've never killed anyone or nicked a person
who didn't deserve it. Sometimes the sins you haven't committed
are all you have left to hold onto.

I might have accepted my fate as a misfit had it not been
for my cousin John who dragged me into a gin-heavy paradise
called the *Zanzibar,* a hot nightspot that had been serving
the local queer community in Ft. Lauderdale since 1951.
The décor had a riverfront brothel vibe. The lounge area,
Illuminated by red-dimmed lighting, was adorned with French
Provincial furniture and a gilded mirror. The etched tin ceiling
featured a disco ball, and of course, the centerpiece was a large
statue of David with a boa.

The bouncer, Al (short for Alice), was a leathered butch
who ignored my fake ID, sensing that I had a need to belong,
to be accepted. She sized me up as a nerdy bookworm,
led me to the back room where her long bookcase full of gay
and lesbian literature lined a wall. As a former English teacher,
Al introduced me to books of poetry— Audre Lorde,

Adrienne Rich, Minnie Bruce Pratt, gave me a tiny flashlight
so I could take a seat at the back table and read. And I read, and
I memorized, consuming poem after poem, until I began to only
speak in poetic verse. I became a Zanzibar regular
in the afternoons. People would ask, how was your day?
I'd answer with a Dorothy Parker quip, *"I never complain,
I never explain."* And when I couldn't find poems that mirrored
What I was feeling, I began to write my own.

One night I told Al what Miss Peale had said to me,
and she replied, *Heterosexuality is not normal, it's just common.
Let me give you some advice,* she said, *Motherfuckers
think they can mess with you, but they can't kill the Bitch.
They might fuck her up sometimes, but, nobody kills
the motherfucking Bitch. You know what I'm saying?*

I reckon her words set me on a path, to live my life
authentically. Taking pride and pleasure in the fact
that we're all unique, I learned to stretch stanzas, fold
back images on one another, and bring someone else
along with my stories. Al also reminded me not to squander
words, or toss them like pennies in the air– but to treasure
the voice that builds bridges toward a new tongue.

Domestics and Hired Hands

The Newsboy

In 1953. my paper route was lassoed by the redline,
serving the working Black, the elderly, even the poor
who live in tarpaper islands, the old healer woman
who hung medicine roots to dry over her wood stove.
I can still picture it all.

In the afternoons, I pedal past white birches,
breathe the smoke of spring chimneys, my heart
pumping uphill toward someone hungry for word
of the world. I am Mercury, bearing news, my wings—
a single-speed maroon Schwinn bike, purchased
with my earnings. I sear a bright path through Churchville,
Orchard Knob, Lincoln Park, and Scruggstown,
to the sick, the tired, and the lonely.

Sometimes at dusk, I sneak into the city
behind the skyline, up steel grids, past the factories'
last hot breath that pushes itself everywhere like a stain.
Downtown, they start to come out, the white men
in black suits who can't wait to loosen their ties.
They brandish briefcases like tense dreams that repeat and
repeat. Secretaries exit buildings alone, their white gloved
hands cupped as if in Methodist prayer.

At five o'clock, everyone wants bourbon, the *Times*,
and sleep. Businessmen pass me, muttering, "go on
back home, boy." Salesgirls rush to the bus stop
with a smell of old gardenias, stiletto heels clicking,
stockinged legs, nylon against flesh, swishing like castanets.
On street corners, newspapers hide faces. Headlines
turn the whole world into one small idea. The old drunk
propped on the corner is asleep with a smile on his face
that could save this city.

When papers are delivered and sold, my wire basket
empty, I part the blue darkness toward supper, confident
I've quenched this day's thirst, stronger in the knowing,
I ll be needed again tomorrow.

Most Southern Ghosts are White

Most fancy Southern hotels have a ghost,
either a Confederate colonel wailing over his doomed
ideals or a gauzy debutante searching for her date
to the Cotton Ball. Some guests check in and never
check out. But where I clean at the Read House Hotel,
it's all about Room 311, where the spirit of poor Annalisa Netherly,
who was allegedly beheaded in the bathtub by a jealous lover,
haunts the suite. There are other ghosts at the Read House, too.
I can attest to that. Luckily, it hasn't amounted to much more
than tingling touches, unusual shadows, whispers,
and maybe a joke or two.

Before I start to vacuum Room 311, I check closets,
under the bed, and behind the shower curtain, carry
a bottle of Pledge cocked and ready to defend. I saw *Psycho*.
Who in their right mind takes a shower without a paring knife
in the soap dish? Personally, I've never witnessed a specter,
but I've heard they hang in hotels frequented by rich white folks.
What is up with that? I mean why are benefactors of apparitions
mostly white and wealthy? I heard Savannah alone has 100 ghosts
who at this moment are standing at the top of spiral staircases
in bourgeois inns.

Who ever heard of a haunted Black hotel?
Chattanooga's Martin and Grand might have hosted
the likes of Cab Calloway and Muddy Waters, but no poor
ghoul with a broken heart has ever been spotted walking
their long hallways for eternity. I suppose it's an entitlement thing,
like the family silver that Miss Scarlett hid in the root cellar
when she heard, *Yankees are coming*. If you're rich in Chattanooga,
you get a poltergeist and a mink stole, maybe, a gold Buick.

We do acquire ghosts in the Black neighborhoods but
we must earn them — kill somebody to get one; none show up
without cause. My grandfather claimed he saw Black banshees
on moonlit nights when he took a stroll through the Confederate
Cemetery on East Third Street. My grandmama declares the number of
sightings were in direct proportion to the amount of alcohol
he consumed those nights. Funny how the spirit world
comes into focus after you've had a few.

Clearing a Black Cemetery

I glance at the jagged glass, embedded in two
arching cedars, a makeshift cemetery gate for unmarked
graves, hidden among debris and dereliction, covered
with brush. Fieldstone monuments spread out like haphazard
constellations, as if they had been back-swiped by the devil's
impudent hand. All of it gives me pause to shiver, wonder
what it would be like to be dead in a place like this.

I feel a presence and turn to find a thin-framed
man; shoulders rounded up by time, like he's perpetually
shrugging something away-- a worry, a compliment
or a question too big to answer. His hair has aged gray,
though his brows hold out, almost as dark as when he was a boy.
In one hand is an axe, chain saw in the other. *Morning, Ma'am,*
he says, and then begins tearing weeds and vines smothering
tombstones, choking memories, burying the dead, again and again.
Giving no explanation of his actions, he continues as if nudged
by some force much greater than a paycheck
or mere human motives.

The next day, he brings a folding chair so I can sit
and keep an eye on him as he hacks away at arm-thick vines
and drags rotten branches from the graves. Soon the darkness
of the place lightens and I can see he is carving out his own path,
dragging away his own debris, uncovering earth that hadn't seen the
light of day for decades. There is something else at play,
that unknown element complicit when a person commits to an act
beyond standard human kindness—that mystery of service,
the ineffable arithmetic of someone giving and giving of themselves
until they are both nearly gone and, somehow,
even more fully alive.

Everyone needs a good clearing, rooted in tenderness,
to open life's veins, where darkness no longer shields
the past or turns humans into animal prey, where darkness
is but a ghost of an idea, barely remembered, a most estranged
prayer, where our lingering ears are torn from shreds
of forgotten years. That much is clear.

Pressin'

My mama calls it "doing the pressin,"
and you know how right she is. Something's urgent
about a hot iron. I can still smell hair burning in the kitchen,
and the fiery straightening comb that gives off a *hisssss*
as Mama smears on Lucky Brown pressing oil, still feel
the dead stillness of my body, praying silently "Lord, spare me
a burned scalp." But for time's sake, Mama wasn't always
gentle. Beauty is not without pain for little Black girls
who are taught straight hair is prettier, easier to manage,
and less threatening as we strive to squeeze into thin white illusions.
I can still see her slender waist, the curve of her neck,
as Mama lays flat the tangles of my unruly hair. The heat
in our kitchen made us glow those mornings. She always smiles
apologetically as I wince, the iron scorching my brow.
Sweat glistens above her lips, her face strangely beautiful,
as only suffering can do.

I remember the time she took me with her to work
at Mrs. Daniels house. It was a sweet day, the kind you'd like
to press between pages of a book, or hide in your sock drawer,
so you could touch it again. At the ironing board, she turns up
pocket corners, picks out the dark lint that collects there.
I imagine she's tempted to leave it, press over it, but old lessons
go deeper than human frailty. Not even the hiss under each
button or the yellow business ground in at the neck can render
trivial one instant of her work. I can still smell the odor of sweat
rising as she pushes steam under the armpits, the owner's
particular smell she could never quite wash out.

For decades my Mama bent over washing, mending
and carrying tubs of water to bathe other mothers' children,
cool-rag their fevered faces. Once home, she bent over
her husband's back, her veined callused hands kneading
his work-hardened muscles. Last week, she cut up a few of daddy's
old suits, humming as she sewed and pressed a decisive stroke
down the long sleeves that ended with a permanent edge
on a traveling outfit for my trip to college, the long bus ride
that will separate us for the first time, my face pressed
against the glass window as I wave her goodbye.

So What

After gardening in Mrs. Spencer's yard for twelve
hours,my daddy wou ld put on Miles Davis' *Kind of Blue*
when he got home and holler me into the garage.

Hear this, boy? One, four, five. That's all they play.
Sons o' bitches. . .

I never understood how any man could break his back,
hour after hour, come home and listen to Miles Davis
for another three. We usually split a 40-ounce Colt 45
when "So What" came on.

Daddy sings the words that Miles didn't need, Coltrane
fading in after Miles' solo, then Miles is gone— not allowed
to come back until the end. Those are the rules.
My daddy taught me that. Rhythm section keeps time
like running water-- brush stroke, snare off, over and again.
Coltrane catches a wind of the last phrase, echoes,
and goes off in his mind wherever it was he went off to:
possibly a cooler full of crappie, a sharp cleaning knife,
fish guts on his glasses and collar, in his hair glinting blue,
playing "So What" instead of recounting a fish story.

Southern Exposure

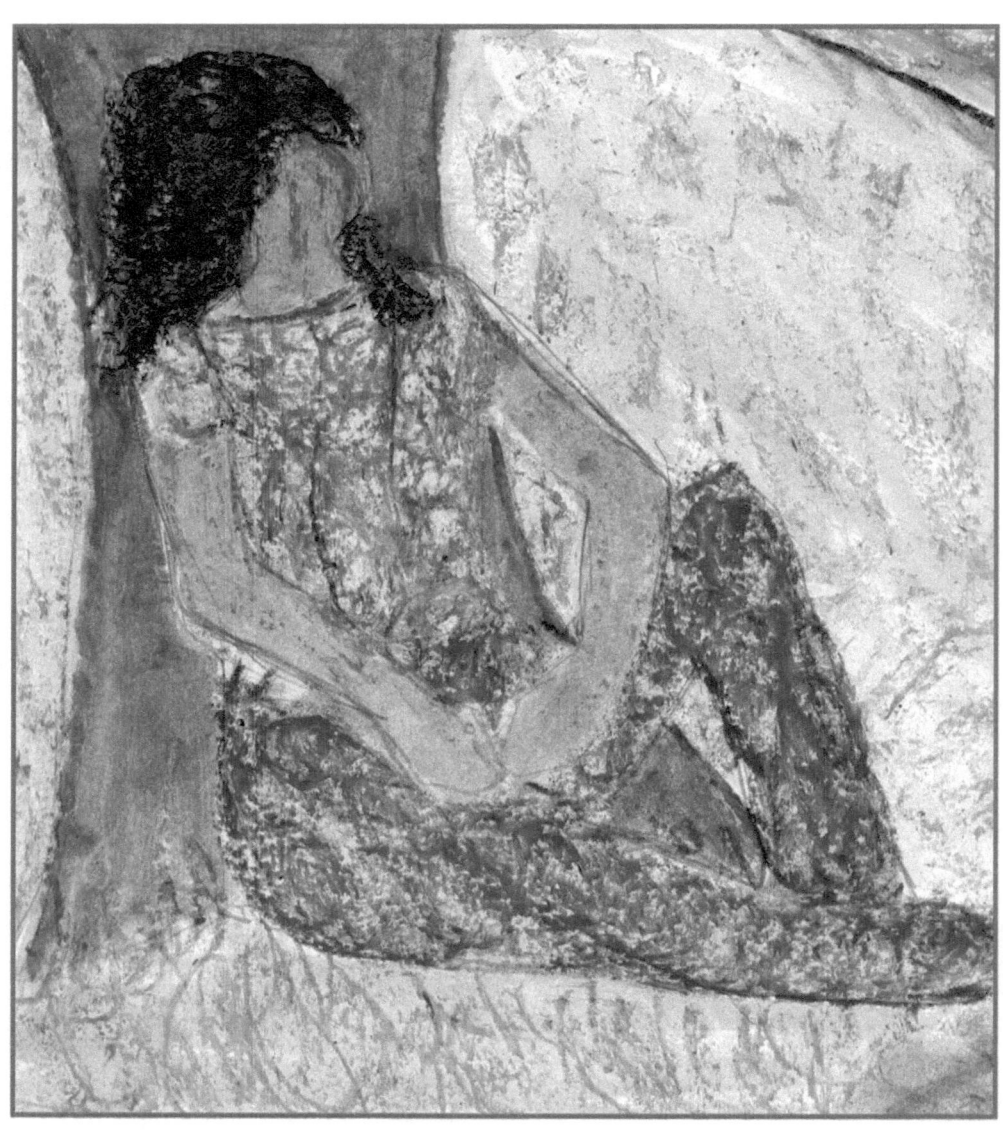

Home

Let me take you back to 1951. Chattanooga —
land of tourist amusements-- natural wonders
like *Rock City* and *Ruby Falls*, roadside animal farms
with bears in cages and tourist traps on Cummings
Highway like *Pete's Cider Barn*. *"You're almost there…*
here it is… "You done missed Pete's," chides the signs
as your car whizzes past the entrance.

I can still see it-- long about August, summer specializes
in time — slows it down to almost a dream. In downtown
cafes, Coke water rests in uncollected tumblers, businessmen
dressed like Joe Friday on *Dragnet*, take up afternoon napping
behind closed doors, and secretaries tiptoe in stocking feet
along linoleum floors for any reason to create a breeze.

In the magnolia-shaded houses, silver-spooned white
women recline in upholstered loungers, smoking their Virginia
Slims and browsing *Sears* mail order catalogs as black women
finally take a seat at ironing boards and leftover meatloaf
to watch the Lowell family create havoc on *As the World Turns*.

Out on the farms, Wonder Bread families shell peas
and shuck corn with mosquitoes and flies on sultry front
porches while pockmarked fields bloom litter and weeds.
Summer vacationers, bound on long, hot daydreams to Florida,
zoom past our windows, spinning the day over and over,
until tomorrow settles exactly where it began.

Clothesline

I was raised in a house without air conditioning.
In springtime, the indoors and outdoors collided.
That's when the scent of hung clothes, peach
blossoms, and fresh mowed grass sift
through window screens, along with the sounds
of nest-building birds and small children playing
between fresh washed sheets. I sometimes saw young
mothers hanging clothes on their droopy lines
as haphazard as their lives — artless. Petticoats, girdles,
stockings, and garters flailing in the breeze for
everyone to see. That's not how it's done.
Big things hang on the ends — sheets, towels, and
bedspreads-- where the line is highest.

A lost art, hanging clothes. All whites go together,
colors hang separately, don't pin shirts by the shoulders.
Pray for sun on Mondays, iron on Tuesdays. Maybe you
think, all this is too domestic for poetry, but have you
seen how dresses dance in the sun,
each to their own rhythm, how the bells of skirts
capture the wind, how blouses strike poses,
side-by-side, as if acting out their different lives.

I can't help doing what Aunt Fanny taught me — starting
from the ringer, we carried loads of wash up from the
basement in scratched white dishpans
to four slick, bleached lines, waiting for us like skeletons
holding out for muscle. We slapped straight, hung,
and punched our clean work in the shape of our years and
waited for the sun to dry it. Even now, though
I have my own washer and dryer, when I open my
windows in the spring, out of nowhere, the fresh
scent of bleached linen cascades
into my kitchen and hollers me back home.

Forsaking Mama's Garden

Oh, how we could dream life, Mama,
as if we were celebrities in *Life Magazine*,
like the one with Doris Day on the cover,
May of fifty-nine. You held her face next to
mine, poofed my hair and patted my
emerging bosom.
Rocking back, you raised one brow to study my potential.
Child, it's a struggle to grow up Southern and sexy,
you'd say as if my garden was already sown in place
with a field full of weeds to hoe.

But I ended up in Berkeley, foggy nights with a
lover who threw bricks at cop cars and walked
midnight streets on psychedelics, measuring time by
fading colors.
We cooked dinner in the morning—pinto beans in a pot
on a two-burner stove, never talking of marriage and
children. Sometimes, I peeled the curtain from the steamy
kitchen window as the sun rose and pictured Doris
weeding goosegrass by your side.

So I called you from that pay phone on
Sundays, across three time zones, to breathe
our thick air, all the while, rifling for that
root of sameness burrowed into our bones.
Me in a glass booth,
sipping Boones Farm from a jelly jar on Milvia
Street, one hand pressed against the free ear to block
out traffic while you told me all about Sissy's
debutant dress
and left your thistles to grow.

Yes, Please

It was a Saturday. Whether sunny or cloudy, hot
or cold, I can't say, but I do remember it was a Saturday
because Mama was off work and downtown was packed
with back-to-school shoppers. She is short, skinny, my mama.
Easy to overlook in a crowd simply because, well,
there was nothing extraordinary to see.

On that day, we ride the bus to town. Strolling down
Market Street, we peek at windows in fleeting glances
because we both know what's waiting in her purse-- the few
dollars and change. I look up at the pretty ladies we pass.
They strut in five-inch heels that click glamorously on the street and
glow in bright, elaborate clothing, faces clear of wrinkles — wiped
away with expensive creams.

An uneasy feeling starts to settle in my chest. I try
to push it out, but it takes root, refuses to be yanked up
and tossed away. It's getting heavier with every second
until I can deny it no longer; I … I am ashamed of my mama
as we stroll into Loveman's where high-class women coo
over evening dresses and mink coats.

I glance at the elegant ladies, then turn accusing eyes
on Mama, study the heavy lines around her mouth,
etched deep into her skin without luxurious lotions to ease
them away. She's wearing cheap clothes with torn seams,
shoes with soles worn down. Her eyes tired from working
long hours at the mill to make ends meet and her hair
much too gray for her age.

I look at Mama and shame comes over me. As she
ambles into the children's department, I hurry away
to the bathroom to hide my face. Finally, making my way
back, I find her standing in the middle of the floor, holding
a sweater that looks much too expensive.

"This will look good on you. Do you want it?" she
says.

Just as I'm about to say, "no thanks," carelessly,
thoughtlessly, I take a closer look at the small, weary
woman with a big smile sweeping across her face
with an outstretched sweater in her hands, thrilled
to be giving me something so nice.

The dismissive words die in my throat. Suddenly,
my mama is beautiful in my eyes. I am no longer ashamed
of her, but of myself for thinking she was anything
but wonderful.

"Do you want it?" she repeats.

With a repentant smile, I answer, "Yes, please."

Mama's Night Out

Mama always said, *Life's too sad to wear*
cheap mascara. Once a week, she divorced
herself from the unlaced *Keds*, crying eyes
pasted shut, hair tied back with a plain rubber band,
the print housedress that bore the stains of her life:
blueberries, blood, and bleach. It could all disappear
with the paints and polishes in four mysterious
dressing table drawers and a three-way mirror.

I can still see her pull on sheer nylon stockings
and black high heels, before studying her reflection.
In the depths of the drawers sit little white jars
with pink tops and tiny roses, high-domed boxes
of face powder that blow *Heaven Scent* across the room
when she cracks the lid, pearl-covered compacts
that snap shut with a glamorous *click*.

When her canvas is covered, she drapes it
with a simple black shift and disappears.
She doesn't look back, not even once, not even
to whisper my name. I imagine her meeting
a *brown-eyed handsome man* in the Green Room
of the Read House Hotel, sipping fine wine
over titillating chitchat.

Years later, I learned she carried herself
to the movies those nights, leaving me to wrestle
with it all, pleased she found romance and jealous
at the same time — of what, I still can't say.

The Elders

Anthony Crutcher

I am a mathematician in spite of the white teacher
at Central High school in 1967 who assumed Black
students couldn't do math. I could have told her
that we brought this skill from Africa when we were
subtracted from her shores, added to a system
of forced servitude and divided as property for over
400 years. We were the multiplier of American wealth
but seen only as a fraction of a human being.

When I was a child growing up in the Bozentown
neighborhood of Chattanooga, sheltered in blackness,
it was easy to live in what I couldn't see for a while.
Such is life: just because there's a warm breeze in January,
doesn't mean a storm isn't brewing. And it came shortly
when I was bussed to Central High School, where the arithmetic
of skin appeared, and the racial shelter of my childhood
was reduced to zero.

I looked for a teacher like the ones I had at Orchard
Knob Jr. High and was met with silence, which is different
than folks saying nothing, like the sound of smoke mistaken
for silence. The teachers at Central High were saying everything
when they actually said nothing. Covert racism in the classroom
was evident in the Moms Mabley joke during the Civil Rights era.
Teacher said, *white boy spell cat... white boy spell rat...*
Little colored boy, spell chrysanthemum.

My second year, all hell broke loose from the white
students after Dr. King was assassinated. Klansmen
appeared outside our high school. White boys yelled,
We killed that nigger King, and you're going to be next.
The only ally for Black students was the custodian,
whose face was compassionate but sad, having missed
equal opportunities by large fractions. Nevertheless,
his door was always open with a lunch to share.

Throughout college, Black students were broken
down like quadratic equations, our squared roots cut
in half. Despite math professors who found me wanting
compared to my white counterparts, I persevered

as I have a gift for solving problems. If train A leaves
Chattanooga at 9 am, traveling at a fixed rate,
I know when it will meet train B. But there were moments,
like being denied into the Ph.D. program in Economics
because of the color of my skin when I wondered
if the trains would crash; picturing my torn limbs
through Pullman windows, each a small vignette
of a frustrated linear equation. I knew X, or thought I did,
shuttled it back and forth across the inequality sign.
The unknown was not always solvable, even to a brilliant
mathematician looking for answers to what I thought
were questions.

So I quit looking for answers and decided to live
the question, and when I come to a fork in the road,
I choose one, like a huge gentle black dog who takes
a bite out of every bark. I've learned to live one day at a time,
through 35 years at TVA, teaching yoga and owning
my own studio, married happily to my sweetheart for 44 years
with two beautifully successful daughters. Just like math,
yoga is also about problem solving. It transforms anger
into beauty. I can't go through life not liking people
because they didn't have to work as hard or come as far
as I did. These days, I still dream in numbers but I prefer
to add rather than subtract.

Dollie Hamilton

Isn't it funny?
That when white folks ask us
about black lives, they assume
we'll automatically talk about our pain,
as if the joy in our stories is accidental.
Or maybe they expect to see my mouth
wide open in wild protest, as if my voice
could flattened a fence, tear a tree apart
in the course of my thundering tongue.

I have been a Black woman
for a long time, and my story is not
about pain or protest; it's about speaking
simple Truths. Beware my smile, I am treacherous
with the Truth. I've been told to lose my attitude.
Ha! As if it wasn't already encrypted into my DNA
by a mother who refused to abandon hope
when her husband touched a live wire and was
electrocuted on the job, leaving her with eight children
to raise—a mother who spoke up and made sure
all eight received the opportunity
to earn college degrees.

I am the Truth Teller who hoists the curtain
to show the underdog's plight; when everything
seems certain, but nothing at all looks right.
I was taught by my mother, "Speak your truth,
even if your voice shakes." And if a kind friend says:
"Be nice," tell her, "Thanks, I hear you. But I will speak
my truth anyway." Women in my day were taught
to please. But truth must not give way to comfort.

The truth is neither positive nor negative,
though sometimes honesty rattles the faint-
hearted, like the time I asked why my children
had no homework at Westview Elementary, or
spoke up for the Black boarding student at Baylor
about to be expelled and sent back to New York-
that kind boy we took into our home, or the time
I was part of a quota in a company whose HR
department was limited to one black professional

at a time. But here's a truth I'm happy to report.
When my husband and I started our own downtown
business in 1987, three Chattanooga banks offered
business loans to support our venture.

I appreciate my white friends who say they feel
sad about how blacks have been treated the past
400 years, yet some caution me that change does not
occur overnight. I chuckle to myself and remind them
that 400+ years is hardly an overnight effort. I also
heard it said, "strong Black women will save us all."
Ha! What a burden to bear. What a falsehood.
It is not my job to save us all. I don't want to be a star,
but part of a constellation.

Listen close. Don't fear. Mine is not a small voice
you hear. I work, pray, try to behave, but that mouth,
oh that mouth of mine, causes a lot of good trouble.
Have no doubt. Mine IS a loud voice that has no fear.
Make no mistake though. Mine is also a love-colored
voice, a loud love you can feel. Though truth may hurt,
I cannot live in gloom, as my mind is fashioned
for hoping and my heart seeks a world in bloom.

Dr. Everlena Holmes

I guess you could say, whenever Challenge came
to the front door, I let him in. How could I not answer,
when Caring followed close behind. For 89 years,
Caring has helped me, gave me an image of human
tears watering the world's gardens. Caring taught me
about Truth, which I have told in writing and at lecterns.
Often. I have cried out against the crimes perpetrated
on the oppressed and marginalized. I've taken a front seat
to witness and protest the mistreatment of the incarcerated.

Since I was a young girl in Tuskegee Institute, Alabama,
I have been planting words in every window box I could,
poking them to become strong. Hoping they'd ignite a fire
that warmed someone. I've planted a garden of strong seeds
across this country. How could I escape them? They follow
after me. Numberless are the kitchens I have sat in,
but our histories of words cannot be eaten. I urge
people to raise their voices and vote.

One vote is an opinion, with a quiet legal force,
a barely audible beep in the local traffic, a drop of mercury
in the national thermometer, but a collectivity of votes —
a flock of votes, a pride of votes, a thunder of votes
can make some noise. One vote begets another
if you make a habit of it. You might say, "What's a block
vote against steam shovels?" These days, a lot of folks
are feeling alone and helpless. "What's the use," they say.
Then the silence comes. It swings back and forth between us
like a rope over a lake, hangs between us like the crowd
above a player not moving on the field, or the quiet
of the day far from the roar of the sun. Until I break it.

One vote was all I wanted in 1958, when my constitutional
right was over 91 years old. When I tried to register, I was literacy
tested, poll taxed, and turned away three times. We used to sing
a song when we marched among towns in Alabama:
    Ain't gonna let nobody turn me 'round,
    turn me 'round, turn me 'round, Ain't gonna let
    nobody turn me 'round. I'm gonna keep on a walkin',
    keep on a-talkin', marching up to freedom land.

I am often asked if I was ever afraid when refusing
to retreat and stay silent. I just tell them, *I make noise*
for the Lord who wants me to rejoice and play horns, drums,
and bawdy noisemakers to beat the band; bang away; speak
of others' uncountable suffering. I believe living as a silent
flower is not worthwhile. On the sacred branch of my only voice,
I insist on justice. Insist for us all, which is the job of the voice.
Else what am I for, what use am I if I don't insist?
There are messages to send, gatherings and protest songs
to sing. We all need to insist. Else what are we for?

Moses Freeman

No one leaves home, unless home chases
you away, unless home shouts at you to quicken
your legs, leave your family and friends behind, forget
pride, survival is more important. No one leaves home
until home is a sweaty voice in your ear saying-- leave, run
away from me now, you know that anywhere
is safer than here.

In 1953, my paper route was lassoed in
by the redline. I was Mercury bearing news, my wings—
a single-speed maroon Schwinn bike, purchased
with my earnings. As a newsboy, I seared a bright path
through Tannery Flats, Blue Goose Hollow, College Hill,
Cameron Gill, and East and West 9th Street. Sometimes
at dusk, I'd sneak into the city, up steel grids, beyond
the factories' last hot breath that pushed itself
everywhere like a stain, careful to stay clear
of the cop who beat me good for daring
to hang out with white boys.

After college, I offered my talent and grit to employers
without reservation, to share without equivocation. I also
led sit-ins and crossed picket lines, integrated thirty businesses
in Chattanooga. It was the first time I believed racial justice
was attainable, that love could replace greed, and people
could live and work with mutual respect for one another.
But white power thought otherwise, laid down an ultimatum---
choose between activism and my job. So I did.

Weeks passed as I wore down leather soles, thinking
my analytical skills and excellent writing would secure
a modest position. But no one in Chattanooga needed
an uppidy Black man who made good trouble. How flat
those words sound, and heavy. My purse thinned
as I tried to keep up appearances and mask
the desperation that thinned my wallet and tightened
my throat. No one leaves home unless home hounds you,
sets fire under feet. It's not something you ever think
of doing until a blade burns threads into your neck,
and even then, you carry the Tennessee anthem

under your breath, only tearing up your voter registration
card when it's clear you won't be going back.

So, I moved to Florida to work for 10 years. But eventually,
I missed the mountains and pines of Chattanooga, and
returned to the battlefields where Black troops fought and died,
where monuments are named to honor the Confederacy,
and where I continued fighting for equal opportunity and fair
housing. As a city councilman, I worked toward the day
where Black children are born and raised in world
that does not reek of poverty and hardship.

In some ways, my life is easier in old age. Gone
are the days of constantly wrestling the problems
and oppression encountered in my youth (though, strangely,
as I age, I feel less and less seen by the young as a force
to be reckoned with). My skin certainly got looser, my middle
rounder, even lost a leg to slow me down just a bit. But
I've experienced enough of life now to know that all change
is difficult, especially when you want it, even when you know
it's good. And change, after all, is what the movement
was all about. Changing Chattanooga. Changing
relationships between white people and those of color.
Changing myself, for sure.

Mimi Nikkel

This is my story, a hundred times over.
It pains me to tell you of it, but I promised
to tell the truth. Don't fret. It can't hurt you,
or me anymore.

Who told you to touch me? Who told you my body
is for sale? I DID NOT! I was only a child
when I was targeted. Sold at age nine. My sweet,
innocent heart and body were used by men, satisfying
their guilty pleasures. They gave me money, drugs,
alcohol, and sometimes shelter, but in the end,
they pilfered my dignity and self-respect, tied me
up good with invisible chains.

I once heard it said by traffickers, *I can only
sell a dime rock once, but I can sell a woman
a thousand times.* The condition of a sex slave
confuses morality, I did what I needed to survive--
alcohol to ease the anxiety, pills to kill the pain,
and cigarettes to keep me from being hungry.
And to endure, I wore masks. Longing to be seen and heard,
pretending was an art becoming second nature for me.
I'd I give you the impression that all was sunny
and unruffled. Arrogance was my name
and coolness my game. I needed no one.
And you might have believed me.

But actually, I don't like hiding or pretending
to be someone I am not. I was sitting in a seminar
on Adverse Childhood Experiences at a conference
for women survivors of trafficking when my prison walls
came down. "What happened to me" became more real
than "what was wrong with me" and light replaced the blank
stare in my eyes. So, I surrendered to the reality of complex
trauma and began healing from decades of constant oppression
related to exploitation and fears. It was not easy. A long
conviction of worthlessness builds strong walls.
I fought against the very thing I cried out for.

But the compassion and love of other brave,
strong, healing survivors shattered the stone walls

I built around myself, allowing tenderness to seep
back into my heart. Eventually, I rediscovered the lovely
girl I lost in my childhood.

But my story is not in the past—it reappeared
at the front door in another woman's face and I knew
it was time to give to others what had so freely
been given to me. So I started Love's Arm to help
women survivors of prostitution, trafficking, and addiction
into recovery. Sexual abuse will remain my story
until women from Brooklyn to Oakland can sit back
in amazement and say 'I can't believe such things
ever occurred," until the word 'rape" is wiped out
from vocabularies, removed from the dictionary,
stamped out of our memories, until there are no
wounded eyes to tell it.

Who am I now, you may wonder? I am someone
you know very well. For I am every
woman you meet. Somewhere, always, there's a day
when healing comes. Isn't this what life is supposed
to be after pain--the healing? Yes, I say, healing
will come. And with God's help, we can create
a new story and call it whatever we want.

Pat Wilcox

These days, too many journalists might
well be lumped in with hedge-fund managers,
pharmaceutical lobbyists, and religious
charlatans.

But as a young reporter and opinion
writer in the newsroom of *Chattanooga Times*
from the 1970s through the 90s, I felt accountable
to the public, sticking to the facts in a way
that slid through a reader's brain, straight
to the heart. Capturing a story was like raising
a seashell to my ear and being overwhelmed
by the roar of humanity. The weight of my job
scared me throughout my entire career, but
God carried me through the daily challenges.
What I liked most about the newsroom were
the happy sounds-- click, click, clicking of typewriters;
leather soles on linoleum floors; teletypes;
overlapping voices — the jokes and impressions
of the more colorful reporters.

During my early years at the *Times*, the air
was so dirty, you couldn't see Lookout Mountain.
Racial conflicts and divisions plagued the city,
as did Chattanooga's longstanding culture
of top-down decision making that favored the rich
over the poor. I was aware of disparities and so
I was always looking inside the skin of the news.
What's at the core? What's left for me to discover?
What's not being said?

I learned to listen to the poor and powerless--
hundreds of hearts, housed in bone and driven
by blood, hummed in the city around me.
There were good moments, the kind you'd like
to press between pages of a book, or hide
in your sock drawer, so you could touch them again.
The bad moments, well, my regret is not exposing
enough of the hard truth. Good reporting begins
at the end of your comfort zone.

Modern Chattanooga seems to have overcome
many of its past problems, although racial divisions
and prejudice still exist. Chattanooga is still the place
where social and economic grandeur whispers, *there
are those above and those below, those that matter
and those that do not*. I remain trapped somewhere
between judgment and forgiveness.

While I've had a good life, albeit a privileged one,
it is not without sadness over images of oppression
in this so-called land of the free. I'm frustrated
with the inability of words to stop the hatred, violence,
and injustices. But as long as the opportunities
for my Black neighbors are much more difficult,
I am not done writing. I'd create another ending for
this story if I could — a happy one, like one
where the good guy lives because the bullet struck the
whiskey flask in his pocket instead of his thin- walled
heart. Or one where the girl is thrown
from the wrecked car and lands perfectly on a pillow of
grass instead of the pavement.

But fiction is not the journalist's job.

Momota Ghosh

Yes, I am 98 years old and I still pray,
meditate, exercise, and keep my mind
busy writing poetry, painting, crafting and working
on crossword puzzles. I have a routine. Never
leave my room in the morning without making
my bed. Breakfast is always cereal, banana,
and tea. Then exercises, beginning with
20 squats, and 30 touch toes.

Here's what I want to say to you:
the most important thing for us to do
is love God. You don't have to go to church.
God isn't a religion, it's love. The very reason
we are in this world is to love and take care
of each other. It is important to see God
in every human. If you want peace of mind,
do not find fault with others. No one is a stranger,
my child; we are all one.

My name is Momota and I grew up in India
but Chattanooga is my home and I love it so much.
It has welcomed me for 33 years, and my door is always
open to you. If you visit, I will show you my prayer room
with photos of Jesus and Mary, Buddha, Sarada Devi,
Swami Vivekananda, Ramakrishna,, and Kali. Truth
and virtue are the same in all religions. Love of God
is the essential thing. All else is unreal.

I have felt the weight of stones by those
who would condemn me as an outsider, suffered
the words of those who look down upon me as inferior,
but I say to you, please don't throw stones. Please
don't spread your religion by the use of the sword.
Be open to all religions that spread love. Someone
once asked me, "Mo, do you believe in God?"
I answered, "Sure, lots of 'em."

Work hard to become enlightened. Pearls live
in the deep sea, but we must hazard to find them.
If diving once does not bring you pearls, don't
conclude the sea is without them. Dive again

and again. Set your heart upon the work, but never
on its reward. The greatest contentment comes
from devotion alone and not from its rewards.

We all make mistakes. Have no regrets.
The only true regret is spending your life
worrying about the future. Let go of sorrow
for it is simply longing for the past. Listen to others
with all your heart. The highest pleasure is
to hear a good story. God Bless.

Peggy Douglas, Ph.D. is an oral historian, college professor, playwright, performance poet, and musician with various string bands in Chattanooga, TN. Her poems and plays are borne out of oral history interviews with people from marginalized communities. Douglas is an introspective monologuist and her self-described playwrighting genre is "theater of personality." Peggy has listened to hundreds of people over the years who persevered through difficult circumstances, and she shapes their disparate voices into a collection of poetic monologues, which she then reproduces onstage.

Peggy learned the art of liberatory oral history and storytelling from mentors at the Highlander Folk School in New Market, TN, where they collected stories from Appalachian voices seldom heard, like former miners, millworkers and unsung heroes in social change movements. In 2022, Peggy received the 2022 Tennessee Arts Commission's Individual Artist Fellowship Award for Playwriting.

Her production company, Southern Exposure is the outreach program for Obvious Dad, a professional theater company based in Chattanooga.

https://southernexposurechattanooga.com
https://www.obviousdad.com